After Sunday Mo'nin" Poems by Angela Marie are a compilation of inspiring words of art. The rhythmic flow of her words pulls the reader in and demonstrates a spiritual connection between her inner soul and the realities of life. Through prayer and praise Angela Marie has captured the very essence of God's grace, mercy and forgiveness which are attributes of His existence.

Dr. Wanda Miles Woodruff

Her warm, savory,delectable, edible verses will leave you craving volumes Angela Marie's unique style. After Sunday Mo'nin' will leave you with the satisfaction of having the best Sunday  dinner in the company of your dearest family members and friends. A must read.

Rena Price M.Ed.

Angela has written from the depths of her heart in "After Sunday Mo'nin'." People from all walks of life are sure to resonate with it!

Pastor Arthur D. Taylor and Sis. Rhonda Taylor

*You will be delighted to see how God's presence is evident in every ugly, shameful, joyous, mundane, and real life situation. It is a book about salvation, a gift that is freely given.*

*A. Jones M. Ed*

# After Sunday Mo'nin'

Poems by Angela Marie

authorHOUSE

*AuthorHouse™*
*1663 Liberty Drive*
*Bloomington, IN 47403*
*www.authorhouse.com*
*Phone: 1 (800) 839-8640*

*Published by AuthorHouse    11/16/2015*

*ISBN: 978-1-5049-6219-3 (sc)*
*ISBN: 978-1-5049-6218-6 (e)*

*Print information available on the last page.*

*Any people depicted in stock imagery provided by Thinkstock are models, and such images are being used for illustrative purposes only. Certain stock imagery © Thinkstock.*

*This book is printed on acid-free paper.*

*Because of the dynamic nature of the Internet, any web addresses or links contained in this book may have changed since publication and may no longer be valid. The views expressed in this work are solely those of the author and do not necessarily reflect the views of the publisher, and the publisher hereby disclaims any responsibility for them.*

**KJV**
*Scripture quotations marked KJV are from the Holy Bible, King James Version (Authorized Version). First published in 1611. Quoted from the KJV Classic Reference Bible, Copyright © 1983 by The Zondervan Corporation.*

# Contents

# About the Author

Angela Marie is an inspired writer. She is an artist of words. She has been an educator of children and has worked in public education for over twenty years. She attended Temple University for her undergraduate degree and earned her Master's degree from Grand Canyon University.

Angela desires to uplift, encourage, and lead human kind toward a sober and sound emotional state. She is an intense observer and an empathetic conversationalist.

Enjoy her words and share them.

# Preface

# After Sunday Mo'nin'

Is when my life begins…
Facing challenges…
Looking at myself…
Making applications of my faith
And seeking God's HELP…
As soon as I lift from the pew…
And my thoughts swirl around…
I have to make decisions
About what to do…
Enjoy, " After Sunday Mo'nin' Poems " by Angela Marie☺

Dedicated
to
you,

The Reader…

# My Fig Leaf and Asherah Tree

written 9/23/2015 @ 6:25 p.m.

I have danced under Asherah trees
And hid myself with a fig leaf....

As if God didn't see me...

I've hidden in temples...
With a fig leaf in my hand...

As if God didn't see me...

I have braided my hair
And dressed my face...

As if this fig leaf
Could help me escape...

I've walked out the door
Without addressing the needs of my soul...

Running and not fleeing toward...
The ONE to WHOM can make me whole...

I have carried a fig leaf in my hand
And waved it.
 And held it close to my heart....

As if that leaf
Could reconcile what my sin had torn apart....

I have sung a song
With a fig leaf in my hair…
Knowing and feeling an absence in
my
air…

So…
While I am hiding,
and walking,
and life is rough….

I have to admit
That I have
some
fig
leaf stuff…

I,
like Eve
I ,
like
Adam too…
At times turned deaf to what YOU told me to do…

I miss OUR relationship
The walking through the grass…
I hear YOU calling…
while my feet sprint fast…

I'm making a decision…
And
I'm making it now….
To put this self sought fig leaf down.

I'm coming to YOU…
The divider is torn….

I'm running toward YOU….
My heart ripped and forlorn…

With clothes ripped
 And ashes on my scalp…
I've decided that I need YOUR help…

I am totally acknowledging
 my known and unknown deeds.

I see a vast chasm…
A spiritual need….


I'm removing myself from under the Asherah tree…
And that
withering
and flimsy
fig leaf skirt…

for the fig leaf has no power…
it is inert…

I'm moving and acknowledging that Jesus is LORD…
I'm moving and wanting to know more….

I have dropped that fig leaf….
I'm forsaking that dance and the repeated deeds…
That I've done beneath the Asherah trees….

I know YOU'LL clothe me….
In animal skins…
And cover and cleanse me....
With the BLOOD YOU have shed….

I'm putting my sought after fig leaf down….
and picking YOU up
so that I won't drown…

# Slamming Pots and Pans

Written 9/17/2015 @ 8:08 p.m.

Here I go…..
Walking in the kitchen!
Slamming Pots
And frying chicken!

They make me so angry!
And I can't control my temper!
Why can't they just listen!

I took a moment with my hand on my hip…
And I said…
Oh LORD! What is it?

I looked in the mirror
In my mind you see…
'cause I 'm still in the kitchen frying chicken for my family!

I looked in the mirror and saw my face…
It looked like a troll
An ugly disgrace!

So…. In the crevices of my mirrored skin…
I saw the sinful state I was in….
I saw hidden envy and jealousies in a wrinkle…
I saw a sin I repeated, but won't mention!
I saw in the crevices of my mirrored skin…
I saw my nastiness and then…

I saw my mouth...
I saw profane words come out!
And Then, I smelled a horrible stench...
At first I thought it was my fried chicken!

NO NO NO! It was my attitude...
It was that sinful stench
That nastiness exudes!

I fell on the floor after I turned the chicken down...
I asked the LORD to forgive me right now!

I need YOU Jesus!
To wash me clean!
It is through YOUR BLOOD that I am redeemed!
After I cried and lay forlorn...
And bared my soul to the LORD...

I washed my hands and went back to the stove...
And fried that chicken
And baked biscuits too...

With love and Mercy to exude....

I was no longer angry
With a temper spewing...
It was my spirit that God was renewing....

I want my face and fragrance to be sweet in God's nostrils....

Like the smell of this fried chicken
Flowing throughout my household...

# Vacant Voice

written 9/19/2015 @8:38 p.m.

I sang, Holy Holy Holy Lord God Almighty!
　And they jumped up and clapped
　　And bowed
　　　And praised the LORD
　　　　And spoke in honest tongues
　　　　As they did before!
　　　　And my thoughts were far off
　　　　From the HOLY and WORTHY words that I sang…

Because last night and consistent nights before…
　　　I sinned
　　　　Deep sins
　　　　Against the LORD…

And in the purity of their hearts…
　　　　　Some fell on their knees…
　　　　　And began to pray…
While
　I sang…
　　　My heart was far
　　　　far
　　　　　far
　　　　　　far
　　　　　　　far
　　　　　　　　far
　　　　　　　　　away…

because last night and consistent nights before…
    I willfully
      Indulgently
           Sinned against the LORD…

And when it was over
    And the people were blessed…
        I went home
           And I thought about my mess…
No singing
No organ
No drum
No chords…
Just the quiet VOICE of JESUS and HIS WORD, THE SWORD…

I found myself crying about my singing and lying…
    A hypocrite is what I had become!
      Whilst in my singing, I was unsung…

Then I fell on my face
    And cried to the LORD…"Jesus Forgive me and cleanse me
    outside and in!"

Don't want to play church
    Or
     Play with God…
    Gotta be mindful of where and how my feet trod…"
      Whether heavily or lightly
        But HOLY before GOD!
         I'll sit down for a minute
           To consecrate to HIM…
             So that the next time I sing…
             My praise will join in!

# Erased

written 9/17/2015 @ 744 p.m.

I heard the sermon and I heard it well….
    I heard and understood about abstinence …
        holy matrimony…
          I understood about sanctification and living HOLY….

I caught the glimpses and reprimand …
if my skirt was too short…
      So I stretched hemlines to reach the nape of my foot…

I met this guy and his love and words sublime…
     and I slept with him
        more than one time…

I cried and found myself curled in a fetal position…
    While I cried and cried about the sins I committed…

I knew enough to ask for forgiveness and I prayed and prayed not to
repeat it…
    I heard the sermon and I heard it well…
      In my choices and actions I chose to rebel…
I loved that man and I refused not to embrace him…
His sin … my sin…
I chose not to escape it…

The love and his words and the feeling sublime…
And I slept with him
More than one time…

After the thousandth time, I spoke a word to no one…
Not even to God….
Not even to God…
I felt something flutter inside me…
I checked it out, there was as child inside me….
I spoke a word to no one…
Not even to Guy about his son…

I hesitated about the decision I had to make…
Over my mistake…
I rolled over in pain…
I ridded my body of the baby with no name…
I had it done with tears in my eyes…
I had it done with my skirt to the nape of my foot…
But my baby….
I had questions….
About his looks…
His name…
His soul…
His life…

I was so perplexed…
And I am today…..
But God sent a woman with something to say…
She told me…
And I'll tell you what she said….
"Young Lady.,
Hold up your head!
Jesus died in your stead!
Jesus paid the price for you, your son, and your sin…
He died and arose with all power in HIS hand….
The Blood
The Blood
The Blood of Jesus has cancelled your sin out….

It only makes sense….
Young lady, your sin…
Jesus died for it!

Jesus is Lord and HIS grace powerful not weak…
So, stop walking  and staring at your feet…"

So, twenty years later, I let go of the pain…
I accepted Jesus in my heart and became Born Again…

I gave my baby a name…
And I walk on….
In God's powerful grace…
HE knows my son's name…
And my sin…
HE erased…

# Reconceived

9/19/2015 @ 12:56 a.m.

I entered the doors…
  Underwater….
    I was drowning….
      I told no one….
        I smiled…
      I sat down and listened….
          But I couldn't hear what the preacher was preachin'….
                My mind kept wandering to different places…. like
horses at the races
            I finally put my head down….
                Hoping that I wouldn't drown any more…
                  The worries of my heart in my mind did pour…
A little boy stood up in mime…
    I looked up and started to cry…
      He danced…
    He moved…
      His motions were repentant…
        I cried
        I heard and saw the BLOOD OF JESUS…
          I heard and saw that I needed Christ….
                I heard and saw the void in my life…
I heard and saw the NAME to call…
    I heard and saw the LORD OF ALL…
      I wiped my face and went home again…
          This time asking Jesus to born me again…
    I found hope as the water reached my nose…
      As the water assuaged my sin too exposed…
        I leaned on Jesus to make me whole…
            Whole and clean and righteous and strong…

Through troublesome water, HE IS LORD OF ALL…
So, I owe a thanks to that little boy…
Who ministered that day…
Because my ears were clogged, but my eyes could see…
And through his dance I was reconceived…

# Can Jesus Love Me?

## Written 9/20/2015 @ 12:35 p.m.

Jesus loves addicts too?
How can this be true?
To love someone who is a slave…
To a demonic pull
A demonic crave…
Jesus loves me?

I can't deny the pain when I abstain…
My body grows sick…
My veins start to twitch…
And the desire is magnetic
Jesus loves me?
I need it now to live….
How can Jesus forgive?
Me


He died on the cross for sinners like me…
Not holy…
Not righteous…
But…
 needing to be free…

Yes, Jesus died and arose for me….
With tears in my eyes and drug in my left hand….
I pray that Jesus would free me from this Pharaoh and oppressive
stand…

I dropped it this time and started to run
And screamed really loud......
I PLEAD THE BLOOD!

I ran and ran and ran for help....
Praying that Jesus heard my heartfelt yell!
This time I broke free...
And I am still on this journey...
One thing for sure,
Jesus does love me...

He died for sinners like me...
Not holy...
Not righteous...
But needing to be free...

Yes Yes HE loves me...

# Just a Note

written 9/20/2015 2 12:33 a.m.

I wanted Jesus to see my raw skin….
   And to uncover that layer
and that layer
   and that layer
and cleanse me within…

and HE did….

# It was simple

written 9/20/2015 @ 1:18 p.m.

Nothing happened….
I was sixteen and free…
And I learned that Jesus died for me….
It was simple…

The HOLY SPIRIT drew me and I sprinted to hear HIM…
I rejoiced because my sins were forgiven….

My soul drank the truth and my cleats dug deep…
Desperately panting for the WORD to drink….

I prayed for friends and he gave me that too….
We encouraged one another in the things of Christ…
I am so happy to have HIM and them in my life…
It was simple…

It was the NAME of JESUS that took my hand….
That protected me in every stance….
Saved my soul from a torturing Hell…
And saved me from some unnecessary pain….
At sixteen…born again….

Nothing happened….
I was young you see…
I just believed that I needed to be free…

One of my friends said he wanted to avoid hell…

It made sense to me….
Just to believe that HE died on Calvary….
Just to be believe HE came for me…
Just to believe that HE rose again…
JUST to believe in the power of HIS BLOOD…
Just to believe in the power of HIS love….

It was simple…


It was simple…

# At Every Sunrise

written 9/20/2015 @ 2:51 p.m.

I heard the birdie chirping outside my window…
Like it was singing praises to the LORD…

And I joined in harmony and sang a hymn…
And as I sang my voice went higher still….
My voice floated beyond the windowsill…

I sang a song of God's amazing grace….
I sang a song of God's love…
I sang a song of how HE rescued me…
I sang a song of my personal journey!

I sang a song on this particular Monday!
I sang a song of HIS GLORY!!

Though that bird flew away….
I continued to sing…
I sang and sang and sang….
Straight till Sunday morning and…
Each time I opened my eyes….
I heard that little birdie outside….
At every sunrise…

# When I got home

I felt like butter melting in the crevices of sweetened cornbread as I
climbed into bed...
I pulled the sheets up to warm me...
And I nestled the pillow just right...
And I rested as if it were night...

I felt peaceful and at ease...
For the first time in a while
I felt I could breathe...

This time I chose to turn off the phone...
I breathed freely in my quiet zone...

As I slept I started to dream...
I was singing Yes Jesus Loves me...
I also sang Without God I could do Nothing...
I sang and I sang and the words rang true to me...
And in my sleep a tear slid free...

Then I sat up to watch TV....

I chose not to watch my usual thing...
I chose to watch what brought laughter to me...
>               That's it...
>               There's nothing more...
>               My soul just rested today in the LORD.

# After I sing...

### Written 9/17/2015 @ 9:07 p.m.

I sing on the choir!
 I wear the right attire

I quote scriptures with a quickness
and I'm a master of forgiveness...
     But when I come home....
          I don't sing...
       I don't open my mouth...
             Praises should be filling the innards of my house...

               The bible sits on the table...
                    And I believe that I am able...
                  To bless someone's life...
                     To ease their strife....
          But my conversation on the phone...
             Is never about Jesus Christ and HIM on the throne...

I decided to wean from just doing stuff...
I'm weaning from
playing in dirt...
          and paying attention solely to the length of my skirt....
               I am weaning from NOT praying about situations...
               I am weaning from frivolous conversation...
                    I need more of Christ in my daily living...
                       So that my life is Relationship...
                          And NOT religion...

# Position

Written September 15, 2015 @ 6:52 p.m.

My soul lay humbled on its belly
and today it screamed of hate….
And somehow….
The Blood of Jesus was able to penetrate!

Stopped my lips from breaking a man down…
Stopped me and caused my soul to kneel and bow…

My Soul lay flat on its belly though you see me standing…
My soul lay flat on its belly though I feel myself waning…
My Soul lay flat on its belly
Again declaring that JESUS IS LORD!

My soul's hand opened its clinched fist…
Reaching for help because I couldn't resist…
I wanted a nectar….
I wanted it bad….
I wanted something I wasn't supposed to have…

The BLOOD OF JESUS was able to penetrate
Every
Ill…
Pull…
Including hate….

My soul lay humble…
And I could not forgive…
But the HOLY SPIRIT tugged
and pulled …

with gloves
of kid…

somehow….

Someway….

I pushed to praise….
Then…
I felt an ease….and I freely forgave…

Though I wanted to keep that ol' sinner
hostage in my mind….

I couldn't drink Hate's lethal wine…

Jesus is Lord I continue to declare!
I see and hear HIS presence everywhere!

Pulling me up from my own murky mire…
Healing me from my sin and desire….
Jesus is my ark, my haven….
My soul lay quiet reaching toward heaven…

This is my position…

# After Sunday

written 9/20/2015 @ 3:45 p.m.

After Sunday I was able to stand in front of people and speak…
I was able to stand and articulate my thoughts to a group….
My real thoughts beyond chicken soup…..
I was able to sit and be quiet and listen…
I was able to share or not share my opinion…
I was able to be what I needed to be….
Because on Sunday… I simply heard of God's mercy…
And joined in collective praise…
To laud and honor the
ANCIENT

                              of DAYS…

# Like Esther

written 9/23/2015 @ 8:08 p.m.

I hid myself in the lacings of a queen…
I drank Liquid Authority…
And became drunk with power…
Not realizing the span of my impact…

So like Esther,
in a different way…
I too had to pray…
I could bring life to a people or their damnation…
birth
or
spiritual
eradication
 I
Had
To seek
GOD
With all of my heart….
And in my movements be very very smart…
I
Had
To
Walk in truth…
Not in words of hallow…
Lest I be hung by my own created gallows…
I
Had
To seek
GOD

With all of my heart...
And in my movements be very very smart...
I
Found
Myself
On
My
Knees....
And
To
The
LORD
I
Did
Plead
On behalf
Of
The people
Assigned under my authority...

Once I stopped drinking that power stuff...
I escaped that micromanaging rut...
They didn't know it.... But I prayed for my team...
I prayed for them as if there were a raging war...
I prayed and prayed unto the LORD....
So,
I was placed in this position...
Not just because of my skills in administration...
It was to encourage and pray...
And pull and tug
To save people from being drug...
and dragged
and tormented
 by things in life....
This position is not just to wield my power...
But to show mercy while completing the task of the hour...

# It Wasn't Sunday

9/23/2015 @ 9:35 p.m.

It wasn't Sunday…
It wasn't morning…
But I took a breath
And I started to sing…

Because YOU are KING of kings
And LORD of lords
I lift my voice to adore YOU

Because YOU are KING of kings
And LORD of lords
I lift my voice to adore YOU!

Because YOU are the GREAT I AM
I lift my voice to honor YOU!

Worthy
Worthy!
Worthy to be praised!
Worthy Worthy for real!

Worthy
Worthy!
Worthy to be praised!
Worthy Worthy for real!

# The Fragrance of my Speech...

written 9/24/2015 @ 10:37 a.m.

I took off my hat and laid it down...
And brushed my hair...
And plopped my plumpness in my chair...

I closed my eyes and took a deep breath...
And I thought about the sermon I heard...
I considered every single word...

It talked about forgiveness and love and such...
It talked about living for GOD and not talking so much...

How sad it would be to rant and yell
Of my high-minded righteousness
And position souls to hell...

It talked about forgiveness and love and such...
It talked about living for God and not talking so much...

So I marinated my heart with the WORD...
I got rid of that condescending poised position...
And chose to be quiet and listen...

To listen to God
and to whom I am speaking...
Listening before I start my poisonous and lethal leaking....

Leaking words of a Pharisaical nature...
Spouting spattered dung-like vapors...
Just religious spouts escaping my mouth...

I considered my living and how it speaks…
What attitude does my essence leak?

Is it judgment absent of love?
Is it self -righteous and void of warmth?
Is it putrid and offensive so that souls cannot hear?
Is the liquid clear but abusive
to godly,
itching,
or discerning ears?

I considered my living and how it speaks…
What attitude does my essence leak?

Before I got up and out of that chair…
I turned my eyes inward
And stared…

I needed Holy Ghost assistance…
To rid me of my righteous resistance…

I wasn't aware of my tone of reprimand
And the harm I caused to the salvation of man…

I closed my eyes and took a deep breath…
And I thought about the sermon I heard…
I considered every single word…

I started to cry because of the harm of my stench…
And I asked GOD for forgiveness…

I didn't want to just leave my thoughts in the chair…
I asked GOD to change the scent of what I leak…

So that HIS sweet fragrance is my speech…

# Are You Listening?

### Written 9/24/2015

I ain't playin church no mo'!
   Too much time has passed…
      Playin' and talkin' sass…
         Flittin' and playin' without conviction…
            To my own soul, I need to pay attention…
      Jesus is coming soon.
         Accept HIM and avoid doom…
               Sounds like a Fire and Brimstone
               Sermon…
                     are you listening?

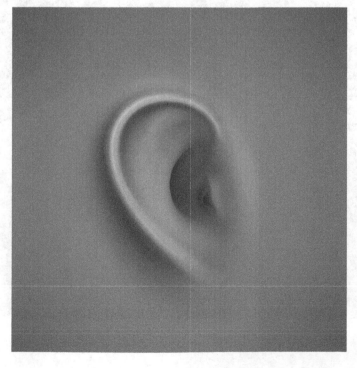

*2 Corinthians 10:5 King James Version (KJV)*
*Casting down imaginations, and every high thing that exalteth itself against the knowledge of God, and bringing into captivity every thought to the obedience of Christ*

# Unseen

written 9/25/2015 @ 3:24 p.m.

I couldn't erase the image pasted on mind….
I couldn't
Get
Rid
Of
It
And
It
Stared at me…

I couldn't unsee what I had seen…
And I couldn't ignore it….
I couldn't make it unseen….

It was ugly and magnetic and it performed acrobatics…
I couldn't unsee what I had seen…
It was ugly and repulsive but it was plastered on my mind…
And
I
Couldn't
Get
Rid
Of
It
And
It
Stared
At
Me…

I couldn't unsee what I had seen...
I needed this monster cast down...
I needed it cast down mutilated and dead...
I need it out of my head...

It was trying to lord my mental space...
It stuck on my brain like a cemented paste....

After I cried and pulled my hair...
The cross pulled me up from sadness and despair...
If JESUS healed Mary Magdalene...
Surely HE could cleanse me...

I saturated my mind....
With the WORD and the victory of the cross...
Believing believing that this image would come off...
I have to say that it took time...
But eventually, I could open my eye....

I couldn't make things unseen or unheard....
But my victory was in the power of the WORD...

HE made it unseen...
HE took away the power that the seen had over me...

Printed in the United States
By Bookmasters